SORRY

ABOUT

The

FIRE

SORRY ABOUT The FIRE

POEMS

COLLEEN COCO COLLINS

BIBLIOASIS / WINDSOR, ONTARIO

Contents // A GOOD CHILD IS COMING *02* /

for Will
who helps me solvere ambulando
& for friends and family who signpost
& for the sweet aandegwag
who show me the verity and beauty
of how the crow truly flies

SORRY ABOUT THE FIRE

A GOOD CHILD IS COMING

More for you,
some coaxed lost wax;

a corner where you
lamp in a smolder;

the learn to expect
to pour it out.

How else to face
        the empty cup

To make it
        lie down
        and gulp, as at

                the dead-eyed dappled horses
                the milk snake's rattle

                the selkie's soft slap-backed paddle.

ALLOMETRIES

No dawnings;
no realizations pricked.
Dross, inauspice;
    limning a pit.

Solitary vertebrates as
seen through slits.

Allometries again:
    stutters, rifts.

(The chassis is unchanged
    but the genesis drifts).

What is manifested in the
middle distance?

A bird at the window?
A car in the ditch?
A disease of astonishment,
    come fast and thick?

A shrieking need?
A keening vacuum?
Periphery as
    a suggestion?

Opposite me: a telamon.

Inside, oh!:   a larch!

I cough in my hand
I land on my back
what cackles and
        brusques me back
        by the collar of my hairshirt

WHAT WAS THAT

what burns that does not
warm the child
what sky today!
shot through with rays

what scattering clamour above
why that
perpetual crouch come out
come out

what pools by my ear
must be spooled out:

I had doubt
I had love
I had doubt!

ATTI E MOTI MENTALI

At the mouth of a hydrothermal vent,
 a quavering current;
  a stent

to the heart of the being
 of the end
  of the death.

I beg your pardon

I might be
 a mountain tiger

and unsuited for this—

I might be a
 bog body

rasped in onto myself

I'm sorry I'm

a bad pennant

drag my length through a
going unrest

bright accost in a puddle

coil unspent

BAWAAJIGAN

Find me in the future:

the hill is steeper,

the dream is deeper.

The water has risen

and is blue.

The way is terraced,

feet are bare,

rushes grasses everywhere.

The people are the throb of

the earth.

Their byre is my

basement.

I am suddenly there too

and then in front

full sun

fully woken into.

BLUEING

The blueing is from the cold.
The loneliness, I'm specifically told, is a predilection
snared in a quincunx of my own making.

Untendered untended unbecoming not-mother.

Flush with nothing; rife with hollow.
Sorrowing through a catalogue of spite.

Indifference, dog-eared.
An always-dripping tap into
an infinity pot.

Where is my salve?
Where

Who approaches,
damp-handed and indifferent?

What reach[ed], slapped back?

BULLISH HOUSE

Poetacademic, in your mournful clench of haught.
Gabled in your mournful,
    in your bullish, trimmed-out house.

Garbled, map-paucit, non-locum, bit-dropped;
yanked rug-ed, caesura-ed; rootless, hiccupped.

Scratching with a dry pen,
counter-hex-divining founts.
Sublimated, as a griddle under
    ever-pouring sauce.

Observe
the diligent
dung
beetle
charting stellar graves /
rolling shit.

CAOINE

when Rose made the recordings

she kept having to be asked

to step back the plosives

were just too much

in the river an oxygen tank

bobs and weaves and gleams

      rings out

struck from without

fast vibrato in the mouth

of the liberating cut

      forced air

      sent out

Rose

keep back   keep back

CIRCULUS VITIOSUS

Cacophony up the flue—
I've conjured a bird again!

Ferret out the instruments of release:
    the towel of appeasal; the mitts of relief.

        Shush the aggrieved.

Make low the panic.
Speak soft.
Widen the window—

Witness: it never was.
    Nothing flitted by.
        There was no distress.
            No almost-crazy-lonely death.

Everyone survived nothing.

COPSE

caesar rabid at
the rubicon

pawing dirt

pawing surf

a pantry on acacia for the shrike/
a copse of death

cleopatra in the dark coiled carpet

[alexa make me laugh]

celtic warrior chews yew

DEHISCENCE

what is love in the mind
of the skidding elephant
irate until the human child
trips into its path

then suddenly most nuanced renouncing colossus.
sudden every thought.
a.
stop.

a bird is born in captivity
too strong a symbol
to be its own

it is so afraid
it has no mind
and not nearly enough torque

again and again
they throw it out
the window but

where else would it go
what does it know
but—

—what is that

it will find our cache
it will find our babi—

there—along the crack:

nunc; comes a seedling
mewly craning   .

who's left open this spigot
of castellated thinking

what astonishes forth
brinkmanshipping

as

love in the mind of the skidding elephant
when the child drops

FAST DROGUES

admit them
these strange arrangements
these fast drogues in the
    name of constancy

pain eater put it aside
that harm dish

you are being welcomed
    to the reveille

everywhere   petrichor

everywhere
turduckens of joy
    and surety

HAUSTORIA

I wanted a good bewildering,
down deep,
as the keep of a castle.

Not cossetted at the perpetual lip!
Not spanning forever the bow!

Make me a lake like for Tiye;
make me a lake I can row.
Make me a lake to run aground in,
and lose under blankets of snow.

Not this fucking about the littoral!
Not *this* down deep,
where haustoria grow!

Not cossetted at the perpetual lip!
Not spanning forever the bow!

HEM

what has been foretold?

      this line will draw
      around this skirt

      the horse is a wardrobe
      full of killers

      and only you know

      the eagle will always
      want the liver

      you couldn't free get tried

HIVES

A smattering of hives,
and a mind torsioned for the new year

like a rising ternion of youth
come over the hill as our lag bolt breaks.

(Stupid children, chiding balk and saving us again.
These peripatetic; these perennial of heart

cranking us home.
And all the while a hot song hissing "fool,"

and I am in the back,
of wind bereft.)

I AM WORKING RIGHT NOW

I was a thousand years old.
The clouds were my daughters;
the eagles occlusions in my eye.

My pulse swamped cities;
snapped the highway up as if
a sheet; shook it free.

I tossed only myself in this.
You settled back at once,
a stone in want of sleep.

I followed a sweet breeze away
but could not shake the quickening cold,
the old skeins.

I stopped crying.

Someone sent the rain to
lash you back
but you slept on in a seethe.

I DIDN'T GO BACK

I didn't mean to step on the snake
that hatched from the soft gloss
of the eggs I touched by accident
beneath the struck half pine

and who may have left crickets
on the basement bed as alms.

IGNIS FATUUS

How fearful and dizzy 'tis!
To cast upon welcome and distance at once;
upon common time lapping
at the shore of the nonce.

To see the puckered suggestion
of a weir out there,
and of a fish eye rolling back
ecstatically into the blue.

Leap up!
In common time and entrainment,
ye un-sessile,
from the bier to the jut—

where live airs;
chants pushed through rock;
Aeolian ventricles as
spanned gone parts.

Natura naturans—
leap up, leap up!
Ignis fatuus settles in
to pluck the gut.

I LEARN BY GOING (THERE IS A FIELD)

All day I set to reaping sheaves

until
stutter / dusk / eklusis /
furl without.

I am as the ruff of the crow in the wind.

Mothaitheacht.

You are as this stooked field.

Lampada tradam,
I am divest,
I go by night.

LILIA

for a moment,
as though through a squint,
the night compressed
and i was in the eye of another.

i did not rise to it,
bewildered as i was,
checking grammar
—making grammar at all—

but when i came to
i was changed:

on the other side of the rampart

unsure whether the hotness of foot
had come by way of lilia or

    flee

META-HORROR-NOIA (A SHARK'S TALE)

Now trumpets mute
as from the head of a pin:

rejoice!
The enemy is not within.

It is de-finned and heaved
over the rim and called
Log.

And now gasps at the bottom
for none to take in:

lost wisdom in the language of
leaching carbon.

NIGHT PLOW

Toothed bucket
come jabbing
through the bank

small thing

shrugged out
from under the aegis
of the sky,

swept backwards
        through death.

Flung, as off the side of a fringed rug.

No tine contrite.

None to hear the cleave:
        the filigree plea, the
        cut.

All patterns arising:

a practical animal

        in an implicit frame

        chunking information.

Spotted wobble in a
        nearly barren tree.

        punted at hard.

        bobbing.

        not/complicit.

NOCEUM CARNAL

fish in the slip
give in, let me cup you up

from the jangly gutter
and its nervy flow

site of the body/
site of the blow

site of the stuttering, peripheral flow

site of that night across the wide footbridge

what whooshes now?

a hard-won lexicon
a crumpled bow

imperceptible theft
subterfuge in the shallows

sudden deluge

controlled issue

fine bones
pre-snag

OBLIQUE

The fox plays dead
'til the moribund crow flies low.

When she told you I was a prodigy
you couldn't let me know.

And they all go into the old pyramid
remarking on the echo.

Now go deeper.

The cupboard faces a wall;
the door is shut.

The fox plays dead.

I'm up in my head
tread, tread, tread, tread,
and you can't hold a candle to this.

The fox plays dead;
the crow swoops.

RADIANT PINE

Behold the radiant pine:
coarse, rural, glowering.

Hunger and discipline/
habit and apathy.

Resolute warp in unmerciful weft.

RESTORATION (1001 NACHT)

Some of us fell in love with steel
and rivets and with cantilevers
and the narrowness of its jibs.

We brought it pizza
and the faith of our mothers
on a spit.

We fucked it in our dreams
and out loud in our
carpeted rooms

where its true majesty could not unfurl
so we cuddled what amounted
to its thumb.

We found solace in the wrist
of the swaying gondola,
as does the kit in the carrying maw.

Some of us toasted it with champagne and came hard and
didn't wash the oil off our faces
when we could have.

RETRIEVER, MÉLUSINE, FLICKER

When I pumped your chest
I had the sudden thought
maybe you had only choked

and opened your warm mouth,
made as if to scoop

a gut of pumpkin out

a stray seed foisted sideways

a clump of unmarshalled anything I could
fist and pitch out.

I managed what came later
beaking in my breast.

Swimming lessons at the neighbour's, 1984:
pool glare, roughness underfoot.

Cricket thrum and bleach and
inundation and 7 Up and

the clack of acquiescence of the board
when the brothers jackknife.

The tale of the bad pact
of the woman fish
who gave it up.

The flicker ate the grubs off above you.
Nothing was meant by this.

(Why was that the deal?
Why did it have to
hurt like knives?)

SNARE HERITAGE

I thought: oh, look at this
bed of pine needles
this soft moss spot

this divot where
the foot kicked out
and was taken up

look at the communicative fetch
of the swinging gibbet

look at the arcing censer
of the death bringer

look at the snow depression there
as under a tree

look at that crater where the
roots pull deeply.

What comes down
through the chokehold
of the apex shape

swaying figura serpentinata
similar but not identical
to contrapposto in that the

lower limbs and torso
face away from one another.

STRUNG

A slipped purchase;
a whoosh back,
woke zoetroping onto event
as facet /
gap.

As punctured bead in a
lightless clasp.

Agape,
ankle-deep in silt:
the first of us, witness
to a new constant:

       burgeon out of morass.
       vade mecum on ash.

       volitional stars, not compliant.

       a weird string, winking into being.

In my mind,
held aloft, :
a miigis shell.

TACIT DYAD

waxwing, small puffed thing

every starling in the murmuration
    faceting

crow in the refuse
        triaging

The heart is a fickle smith,
choosing what it allows to be built.

Craven bight facing jut-out cliff;
sea as emollient,
    roiling to but dint.

THANK YOU FOR YOUR WORK

S:
I saw the essential mushroom
forthing from the ground

each actually legion
the sole an illusion

report back   is there magic

THE BOAR'S HEART

Dark-mantled.
Advancing; trim.
Unlinked; each isled but
    tandemned, and wick-ed.

the heart in my hand is not
her heart
it is a boar's heart
she lives
(I let her go)
the boar is dead
tusks up
in the woods.

Signal as noise,
indistinct.
An irretrievable ground /
    a figure in sit.

FUCK NO THE NADIR

Ball up the literal shit-stained sheets
by the side door.

Clear that out,
that half-frozen intention housing grubs,
the last rites of the dog.

What mattered that you couldn't
let free, what
swelled but curbed?

o fuck,
where is my love

who goes before me
no one
and who comes behind
o fuck
no one i think.

This is the nadir.
The storekeeper glowers.
Our dog dies slowly.
The fire does.

I blinked a _____ quarter-century
and you were gone.

Notes

A Good Child Is Coming is a translation of the Choctaw/Chahta phrase *vlaa achunkma yosh minti*, an expression shared/gifted to me by a friend of Chahta descent.

"a corner where you lamp" is sonically located in Ella Fitzgerald's *Brighten the Corner* album, and Pavement's *Brighten the Corners* album.

"learn to expect to pour it out" is from Margaret Avison's poem "All Out; Or, Oblation," found in my Italian-English copy of *Il Cuore Che Vede* (The Optic Eye) (Longo Editore, 2003).

Atti e moti mentali is a Latin phrase popularized by Leonardo da Vinci, meaning "the attitudes and motions of the mind," to instruct that a more encompassing/embodying representation of the entirety of a person was required in figurative painting and drawing. The line "I beg your pardon [,] I might be a mountain tiger" is written by Ginvera de'Benci (1458–1521), suspected poet, friend, and painting subject of Leonardo da Vinci.

Bawaajigan is Anishinaabemowin for a dream or vision, as encountered in Margaret Avison's *Bawaajimo: A Dialect of Dreams in Anishinaabe Language and Literature* (Michigan State UP, 2014).

The song referred to in "Hives" is Frazey Ford's "Done."

In "Ignis Fatuus," "how fearful and dizzy 'tis!" is a phrase from Shakespeare's *King Lear*, Act IV, Scene vi.

"[W]elcome and distance at once" is from Sandra Sabatini's *The One With the News* (The Porcupine's Quill, 2000).

The line "ecstatically into the blue" is from Heinrich Heine's *The French Stage*. Heine also mentions the bier in his poems "Where? [Wo?]" and "Ascension."

I learn by going is a phrase from "The Waking" (1953) by Theodore Roethke.

Mothaitheacht is described by Diana Beresford-Kroeger in *To Speak for The Trees* as an Irish Gaelic/Celtic word for the recognition within certain people of a kind of dendro-attuned sentience. She writes: "It was described as a feeling in the upper chest of some kind of energy or sound passing through you ... It's possible that mothaitheacht is an ancient expression of a concept that is relatively new to science: infrasound or 'silent' sound."

Lampada tradam is Latin for "I will pass on the torch," and was lit upon in Cole and Hoffman's *The Lost and Found World of the Cairo Geniza* (Schocken Books, 2011).

In "Snare Heritage," the definition of figura serpentinata is taken from Wikipedia.

love & thanks/merci/miigwech/go raibh maith agat to
please rearrange the names of thanks recipients as:
William Kidman, Luke Hathaway, Sheilah ReStack;
Julie Doiron, Shary Boyle, Steven Lambke;
Adam Sturgeon, Jon McKiel, Misha Bower;
Ariel Sharratt, Mathias Kom;
Elders and sages;
& my family (Brenda, Patrick, Marianne, Sean;
& their families).

love & gratitude too
to the brilliant Biblioasis cadre.

love and fealty to the gamboling fox,
the quaking dove, the noble crows,
the clement vultures, the temporal humpbacks,
the vibrating squirrels, the casual bear, the tenty coyotes,
the bending salix,
& the ever-ever-ebbing sea.

About the author

Colleen Coco Collins lives litorally in rural Mi'kma'ki/Nova Scotia.
She also works as a songwriter and visual artist.
Sorry About the Fire is her first book.

A note on the type

This book is set in Signifier, a brutalist interpretation of a 17th century type collection called The Fell Types. It was created by Kris Sowersby and released by Klim Type Foundry in 2020. The display face is Nitti Typewriter, which was inspired by the first sans serif type designs of the 19th century. It was designed by Pieter van Rosmalen and published by Bold Monday.

FIRST EDITION
10 9 8 7 6 5 4 3 2 1

Library and Archives Canada Cataloguing in Publication
Title: Sorry about the fire / Colleen Coco Collins.
Names: Collins, Colleen Coco, author.
Description: Poems.
Identifiers: Canadiana (print) 20230578349 | Canadiana (ebook) 20230578365 | ISBN 9781771966139 (softcover) | ISBN 9781771966146 (EPUB)
Classification: LCC PS8605.O45 S67 2024 | DDC C811/.6—dc23

Edited by Vanessa Stauffer
Cover and text designed by Natalie Olsen
Cover/interior photos © cvrestan/Shutterstock

Published with the generous assistance of the Canada Council for the Arts, which last year invested $153 million to bring the arts to Canadians throughout the country, and the financial support of the Government of Canada. Biblioasis also acknowledges the support of the Ontario Arts Council (OAC), an agency of the Government of Ontario, which last year funded 1,709 individual artists and 1,078 organizations in 204 communities across Ontario, for a total of $52.1 million, and the contribution of the Government of Ontario through the Ontario Book Publishing Tax Credit and Ontario Creates.

PRINTED AND BOUND IN CANADA

Printed by Imprimerie Gauvin
Gatineau, Québec